Q AND A ENGLISH

*Join the mailing list at **palmcirclepress.net** to receive an advanced readers copy of our newest releases. Plus news and contests!*

Q AND A ENGLISH

THE PERFECT PRONUNCIATION WORKBOOK

RORY PENLAND

PALM CIRCLE
——PRESS——

Printed in the United States of America

ISBN: 979-8-9888754-5-1

Book Design by Oladimeji Alaka

Front Cover Image by Subbotina

Interior Layout by Rachel Greene for elfinpen designs

Published by Palm Circle Press
www.palmcirclepress.net

For Tina

TABLE OF CONTENTS

A FEW WORDS ABOUT PHONICS AND PHONETIC

One thing that I have noticed when I am teaching Chinese students oral English is that they can usually read and write English very well, but as there is little opportunity or chance for them to practice their English speaking skills they are reluctant to relax when they speak English. If their teacher was Chinese (most English teachers in China are Asian) they may have learned the pronunciation of their English incorrectly. This very problem has caused many companies and businesses in China to insist on foreign English teachers.

The pronunciation of English words or the way English words sound is called phonetics. Something that is phonic is something that you hear with your ear. Phonetics is the science of sounds: The sounds that makes up words and languages.

Many Chinese people learning English for the first time, struggle with the phonics (fon-iks) and phonetics (fone-e-tiks) of foreign language words. Even more so in China, because we share many of the same letters in our alphabets, but some of them have completely different sounds. For example, the Chinese "E" is pronounced like the English sound "uh" and the Chinese "I" is pronounced like the English "ee" sound.

THE ENGLISH ALPHABET

The English alphabet is larger than the Chinese alphabet. It is made up of twenty-six (26) letters. They are ...

A a	B b	C c	D d	E e	F f	G g	H h	I I
J j	K k	L l	M m	N n	O o	P p	Q q	R r
S s	T t	U u	V v	W w	X x	Y y	and	Z z

The first version of the letter is a capital letter, also called upper case and the second version is the non-capital or lower case version of the letter.

These letters are broken down into two groups. The first group is the twenty (20) hard or solid sounding letters called consonants. They are ...

B	C	D	F	G	H	J	K	L M
N	P	Q	R	S	T	V	W	X
and Z

Y is considered by some to be a consonant and by others to be a vowel (A E I O U and sometimes Y). For the most part, it is used as a vowel in English so that is how I list it in my book.

The basic sounds from these letters are the first sounds* in the following words.

B = Bag	Ball	Bat	Big	Bit	Bug
C = Cap	Call	Can	Cat	Cup	Cut
D = Damp	Dark	Dig	Dog	Doll	Dust
F = Fan	Fat	Fin	Fit	For	Fun
G = Gas	Get	Go	Gone	Got	Gun
H = Hand	Hat	Hen	Hit	Hot	Hut
J = Jam	Jazz	Jet	Job	Junk	Jump
K = Key	Kick	Kill	King	Kit	Kitten

L=Lap	Let	Lick	Lip	Long	Luck
M = Mad	Man	Map	Met	Mom	Mud
N = Nap	Net	New	No	Not	Nut
P = Pad	Pan	Pen	Pin	Pit	Pot
Q = Queen	Quick	Quit	Quiet	Quote	
R = Ran	Rat	Rip	Rock	Roll	Run
S = Sand	Sat	Sing	Sip	Soup	Sun
T = Tag	Tall	Ten	Tip	Top	Tub
V = Van	Vat	Vent	Verb	Very	Vest
W = Walk	Wet	Win	Wind	Wing	Word
X = aXe	fiX	foX	miX	oX	X-ray

(Note: These examples of "X" are truer and better sounds of the letter. In words starting in "X", most times "X" sounds like the letter "Z".)

Xenon	Xerox	Xylophone			
Y = Yam	Yard	Yell	Yes	Yet	You
Z = Zag	Zap	Zebra	Zero	Zig	Zoo

The other six letters of the English alphabet are called the vowels. They are...

A   E   I   O   U   and sometimes Y

These are the letters that really make the words sound the way they do. The way you hear a sound is called phonics. Vocal sound of letters and combinations of letters in called phonetics. In China, the phonetics of these vowels is slightly different than in English phonetics. This slight difference has caused a lot of mispronouncing of words in both languages. If you are learning English and you want to speak it properly, you need to know the differences in the phonetics of the two languages.

I had to learn these differences so it would make my learning of the Chinese language much easier and would help me to be confident that I was speaking the right pronunciation of the words that I would be saying.

In the Chinese alphabet, the vowels sound like ...

A = Ah   E = Uh.   I = Ee.   O = Oh.   and U = Uwa

"Y" in the Chinese alphabet is basically used as a consonant (Yi Yuan) and not as a vowel. In the Chinese language the vowel sounds that we usually hear made by "Y" in English are typically made with a combination of other vowels like "ai" and "ei".

EXAMPLES: (in English and Chinese "Puton Hua")

by, bye, buy = bai   tie = tai.   may = mei.   way = wei

ENGLISH VOWELS AND SOUNDS

In English, each vowel has two sounds. A "long" sound and a "short" sound.

A = The short sound of "A" is the sound of "A" in apple.

OTHER EXAMPLES:

and	ant	bag	back	band	bat	cat
damp	fan	gap	hat	lamp	man	pan
ran	van					

"ai" = brain   chain   drain   nail   rain   raise   sail   snail

"ay" = away   bay   hay   lay   may   spray   stay   today

"eigh" = eighty-eight   neighbor   sleigh   weigh   weight

As with much language grammar, there are exceptions to the phonetics rules. The exceptions to the long "A" sound without the silent "gh" are...

feign   reign   vein

These few words that are exceptions to the rules of phonetics are very rarely used in modern English language so do not worry about them too much.

EXCERCISES:

Circle the words that have the short "A" sound. Underline the words that have the long "A" sound.

Cram   mad   rain   same   bad   rate   train   jam

sat   jail   came   claim   ram   rat   take   crack

The long "A" sound is the sound of the "A" in Came, Train (ai), Play (ay), and Eight (eigh). In most cases, these combinations of letter -- "ai", "ay", "ey", and "eigh" all make the long "A" sound in the English language.

THE SILENT "E"

A silent "e" in a word, especially on the end of a short word, can change a short sound to a long sound. The short "A" of pan, a thing you cook in, with a silent "e" placed at the end changes the word to pane (sounding exactly like pain) which is a piece of glass in a window.

OTHER EXAMPLES:

frame   game   lace

quake   raise   rake

lame   naked   navel   pace   page

sane   save   stake   take

EXCERCISES:

Read the following words with the short "a" sound and then read them again with the long "A" sound as if they had a silent "e" in the word.

can (e)   hat (e)   man (e) pal (e)   rag (e)

rap (e)   sag (e)   tap (e)

Circle the words that have the long "A" sound. Underline the words that have the short "A" sound.

Bait   candle   crate   great   haggle

8

late	main	panic	ramp	shake
taint	fan	half	grapes	past

flat

"A" can also have an "R" sound when it is followed by an "R."

EXAMPLES:

are	bar	car	far	guard
harp	large	Mars	star	varnish

yard

E – The short "e" sound is different from the Chinese "e" sound. In English the short "e" sound is pronounced "eh" as in "wet".

The traditional Chinese sound for "e" sounds like "uh" as in "duck". The Chinese word "wen" is not pronounced like "when" in the

English language. Instead, it is pronounces exactly like the English number "one" or the English word "won". "I won the football game."

The short "e" sound in the English language is like the "e" in the words egg, empty or exit.

OTHER EXAMPLES:

bed	bell	desk	fell	gender
hello	men	net	pen	red
rent	sell	tent	vent	web

The long "E" sound is like the Chinese "I" sound. It sounds like the e's in free or bee.

The long "e" sound is usually formed when the letter "e" is followed by another vowel. Most times this happens when the "e" is followed by another "e" as in the word "teeth"

EXAMPLES:

agree	feet	green	greet	knee
see	sheep	tree	three	wheel

It also has this sound when the e is followed by an "a" as in the word "real".

EXAMPLES:

beads	beak	eagle	jeans	leaf
meal	meat	peanut	seal	sea

The short "e" also becomes a long "E" when followed by "Y", like in the word "money".

EXAMPLES:

donkey	hockey	key	monkey	turkey

If an "e" has an "i" before it, it will usually have the long "E" sound, like in the word thief.

EXAMPLES:

achieve belief	brief	chief	field
grief	piece	relief	retrieve
shield	wield	yield	

There is an important spelling grammar rule in English which will help you. That rule is… "I" comes before "E", except if it after the letter "C". If there is an "i" after an "e" in a word, that will also make the long "E" sound. It is the same as if the "e" was followed by an "a" or another "e".

EXAMPLES:

deceive   conceive   misconceive   perceive   preconceive

receipt   receive

Notice the difference in spelling. If it comes after "C", it is customary to put the "e" before the "I".

EXERCISE:

Circle the words below that have the short "e" sound in them. Underline the words that have the long "E" sound.

pet	been	dent	leaf	bent
repent	teeth	smell	current	tea
fresh	get	left	deal	spend

I – The short "i" sound is the sound of the "i" in "fish". You must resist the urge to pronounce it as "feesh", using the Chinese alphabet pronunciation for it. This is a common mistake. I hear it in my classes all of the time.

Think of the short "i" sound as a very thin sound as in the words "in" and "thin."

EXAMPLES:

bin   bitch   in   dinner   limp

MORE EXAMPLES:

lit   mint   pill   sit   shrimp   tin   twin

11

The long "I" sound is the sound like the word "tire". Most times, the long "I" sound is made by adding a silent "e" to the end of a word.

EXAMPLES:

bike   drive   file   fine   hire   line   mind   mine   pipe

right   shine   shrine   tie   time   vine   wine

However, pairing the "I" with another vowel, will sometimes give it the long "I" sound, like in the word liar.

EXAMPLES:

briar   friar   cried   fried   lie

If an "I" is followed by "gh", it generally takes on the long "I" sound.

EXAMPLES:

bright   high   night   right   sigh   slight

"Y" can also make the long "I" sound, as in the word "cry".

OTHER EXAMPLES:

by   dry   fry   guy   my   pry   spy

EXERCISE:

Circle the words that use the short "I" sound. Underline the words that have the long "I" sound. Circle and underline words that have both sounds.

fire   pin   tie   slide   try   six   kite   lip   pig mild   mice   will   bilingual   die   hinder kind   spry

O – The short "o" sound is like "ah", as in the word hot.

EXAMPLES:

box   clock   dock   doll   dot   fox   got   hop   lock

lot   mop   not   pop   rot   stop   top   wok

The long "O" sound is similar to the Chinese "O" sound, as in the words "no" and "go". As with other vowels, the short "o" sound can become a long "O" sound if it is followed by another vowel (a,i,u) or a silent "e" is added to the end of a word.

EXAMPLES:

boat   dose   float   foe   goat   grope hoe   load

moan   mope   nose   note   pose   wrote

EXERCISE:

Circle the words with the short "o" sound. Underline the words that have the long "O" sound.

block   boat   bone   cross   dog   quote   gross   hop

pot   mope   sock   crow   oxcoat doe   knot   rose

THE TROUBLE WITH DOUBLE "O"S

BE CAREFUL when you see two "o's" (a double "o") together. They can have two sounds. One sound for "OO" is the sound in the words

book   cook   could   good   look   shook   took.

but "OO" can also sound like a long "u" sound, like it does in the words

boo   coo   cool   droop   food   hoop   mood   tool

moon   soon

U – The short "u" sound is the same sound as the Chinese "e" sound. It sounds like "uh" as in the word "uncle".

EXAMPLES:

bum	bungle	chum	dump	fun
grunt	gum	hump	nun	nut
run	sum	sun	tunnel	

The long "U" sound is very similar to the Chinese "u" sound, like in the English word "cute".

EXAMPLES:

blue	buoy	crucial	cube	cue
duel	fruit	fuel	glue	huge

14

mute	suit	tube	use

The long "U" sound can also be made in English words having "ew" or "ou" in them.

EXAMPLES:

crew	few	flew	grew	new
screw	view	rouge	roulette	through

However, in most English words, the "ou" sound is the sound like "ɔw", as in the words

about	astound	bound	doubt	found
pound	round	shout	sound	

EXERCISE:

On the next page, circle the words that have the short "u" sound in them. Underline the words that have the long "U" sound.

bug	busy	duck	drug	genuine
humor	puppy	scrub	truck	tube

THE UNIVERSAL PHONETIC SYMBOLS

sounds like "ee"
REACH

sounds like "a"
BAG

sounds like "ar"
STAR

sounds like "aw"
DRAW

sounds like "oor"
STORE

sounds like "oo"
LOOK

sounds like "ea"
HEAR

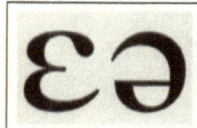

sounds like "air"
WEAR

sounds like "ur"
TOUR

sounds like "oo"
MOON

sounds like "uh"
RUN

sounds like "ir"
GIRL

sounds like "er"
MOTOR

sounds like "A"
GREAT

sounds like "O"
BOAT

sounds like "y"
SKY

sounds like "ow"
MOUSE

sounds like "oy"
TOY

COMMON VOWEL / CONSONANT PHONETIC SOUNDS IN ENGLISH

Ab

"Ab" sometimes sounds like the short "a" sound followed by a "b" sound.

Abdomen	abduct	abnormal	abrupt	absent
absolute	absorb	abstract		

It can also sound like "uh", with the short "u" sound followed by the "b" sound.

abandon	ability	ablaze	aboard	abolish
about	above	abuse	abyss	

Acc

There are a few exceptions to the rule where it sounds like "aks".

accent	accept	access	accident

But generally it sounds like "k".

cclaim	accompany	accomplish	account accumulate
accuracy			

Ach

Usually sounds like "ok" with a short "o" sound as in the name

Bach

Follow it with an "e" and you have an ache with a long "a" sound and a "k" sound (as in bake or lake).

ache   backache   earache   headache

stomachache   toothache

Ack

Always has the short "a" sound followed by the "k" sound.

back   crack   hack   lack   rack

sack   shack   tack

Act

Act almost always has the short "a" sound followed by the "kt" sound.

act   activate   activity   actor   actress

actual   attract   cataract   contract   refract

When the "t" is followed by "ion". It becomes the sound "shun" with the short "u".

action   attraction   fraction   traction

Ad

Sometimes it has the short "a" sound followed by the "d" sound.

adjective	adjust	administrate	admire
advance	adventure	advice	bad
cad	fad	graduate	had
lad	mad	radical	sad

Sometimes it has a sound like "uh" with a short "u" sound followed by the "d" sound.

addition	adobe	adopt	adorn
adultery	tradition		

Af

Sometimes it has the short "a" sound followed by the "f" sound.

affable	affidavit	after	craft	daft
draft				

But it generally sounds like "uh" with a short "u" followed by the "f" sound.

afar	affair	affection	affiliate
affirmative	affliction	afford	afloat
afraid			

Ag

Sometimes it has the sound of the short "a" followed by the hard "g" sound.

aggravate	agnostic	agony	agriculture	
bag	drag	rag	tag	wag

Sometimes it has the sound of the "uh" with a short "u" sound followed by the hard "g" sound.

aggressive   aghast   aglow   agree

Age

If followed by an "e" it has a long "A" sound followed by a "j" sound.

age   agency   cage   page   agent

rage   stage

If it is the last syllable of a multi-syllable word, then it takes on a different sound. The sound becomes "uh" with a short "u" followed by a "j" sound.

carriage   image   luggage   pillage   savage

village

Agi

If followed by an "i" it has a short "a" sound followed by a "j" sound.

agile   agitation   fragile   imagine   magic

tragic

Ah

Ah sounds like "uh" with a short "u" followed by the "h" sound.

ahead   ahoy

Ai

Usually has the long "A" sound.

aid	ail	aim	afraid	frail
laid	maid	sail		
wail	waist			

One exception to this rule is the word "aisle" where it takes on the sound of the long "I" sounding exactly like the contraction "I'll".

If the "ai" is followed by an "r" the sound becomes like "aer".

air	airplane	airmail	airtight	airy
fair	hair	pair		

AL

"AL" is usually the short "a" sound followed by the "L" sound.

albino album alcohol algebra allergy alley altruist

But sometimes it has the "uh" sound with the short "u" followed by "L". This usually happens when the "L" is followed by another vowel, like "e" or "I".

alarm	alert	allegiance	alleviate
alliance	allow	allowance	aluminum

Am

"Am" can sound like the short "a" followed by the "m" sound.

amateur	amber	ambition	ambulance
ambush	amnesia	amphibian	

"Am" can also sound like "uh" with a short "u" sound followed by an "m" sound. This usually happens when the "M" is followed by another vowel, like "a", "e" or "o".

amass	amaze	amend	amenity
American	amidst	among	amount

An

"An" sometimes has the short "a" sound followed by the "n" sound.

analyze	anarchy	ancestor	anniversary
annual	answer	band	bland
can	demand	fan	grand
man	nanny	panic	tan
van			

Sometimes "an" sounds like "uh" with a short "u" sound followed by an "n" sound.

analogy	anatomy	announce	annoy
anonymous	another		

Sometimes "an" sounds like the long "A" sound followed by the "n" sound.

anchor	ancient	angel	angle
angry	anguish	angular	ankle

change	mangle	range	strange	s
trangle	triangle			

Ant

Almost always, the sound for "ant" will have the short "a" sound followed by "nt".

ant	antagonize	antenna	antic	anticipate
antidote	antique	antiseptic	chant	frantic
grant	plant	rant	slant	

Ap

Generally, if the "ap" sound is at the beginning of a word it sounds like "uh" with a short "u" sound followed by the "p" sound.

apartment	apologize	appeal	appear
appreciate	approach	approve	

Sometimes "ap" has the short "a" sound followed by the "p" sound.

appetite	apple	application	apprehend	apricot

This is almost always the case when "ap" is in the middle of words.

chap	collapse	grapple	lapse	mishap
shrapnel	strap			

Ar

The letters "ar" sound just like you are saying the letter "R".

24

arch	are	argument	arm	arson
art	artery	artificial	artillery	aardvark
bark	car	cart	dark	dart
jar	mark	narcotic	stark	

One exception to the rule is when the "r" is followed by an "o" – then the sound of the "a" usually becomes "uh" with a short "u" sound followed by the "r" sound.

| aroma | around | arouse |

The other exception is when the "ar" is followed by another "r" – then the sound of the "a" usually becomes "uh" with a short "u" sound followed by the "r" sound.

| arrange array | | arrest | arrive |

If "arr" is followed by an "o", the "ar" sound is pronounced like "air".

| arrogance | arrow |

As

Sometimes the "as" sound has the short "a" sound followed by an "s" sound.

ash	aspect	asphalt	asphyxiate	aspire
aspirin	asteroid	basket	cast	fast
gasket	hassle	massive	nasty	pass
rash	vast			

Sometimes "as" sounds like "uh" with a short "u" followed by an "s" sound when it is at the beginning of a word.

25

aside   asleep   assemble   assign   assist

assortment   assume   astound

At

Sometimes "at" sounds like the short "a" sound followed by the "t" sound.

atom   attic   attitude

bat   cat   fat   mat   rat

sat   tatter   vat

Sometimes "at" sounds like "uh" with a short "u" followed by the "t" sound.

atop   attach   attack   attempt   attend

attest   attraction

Ath

Usually, "ath" sounds like the short "a" sound followed by the soft "th" sound (as in the word "three").

athlete   athletic   bath   catheter

mathematics   path   wrath

Au

When "a" is followed by "u" it often sounds like "aw".

auction   audio   audience   audit

August   aunt   uthentic   auto   autumn

Av

Sometimes "av" sounds like the short "a" sound followed by the "v" sound.

avalanche   avarice avenue   average   avid

have   gravel   travel

Sometimes "av" sounds like "uh" with the short "u" followed by the "v" sound when it is at the beginning of a word.

available   avert   avoid   avow

Aw

In almost all instances, the "aw" sounds like "uhw" with a short "u" sound".

await   awake   award   aware   away

awhile   awoke

Ax

"Ax" always uses the short "a" sound followed by the "x" sound.

ax   axial   axiom   axis   fax

galaxy   maxim   relax   saxophone

Ay

In most English words, "ay" has the long "A" sound followed by the "y" sound.

bay   day   gray   hay   May

ray	say	stay

Ea

In most cases, "ea" has the long "E" sound.

each	eager	ear	ease	east
Easter	easy	eat	beat	deal
feat	meat	real	seal	seat

In some cases, "ea" takes on the short "e" sound.

dead	dread	head	spread	thread

If "ea" is followed by an "r", the sound changes to "er". The word "ear" is the only exception to this rule.

early	earn	earnest	earth

earthquake	earthworm

Eb, Ecc, Ech and Eck

The sounds "eb", "ecc", "ech" and "eck" all have the short "e" sound.

ebb	ebony	eccentric	echo

check	speck

Although echo has a "ch" which usually sounds like the "ch" in "Chili", it sounds like a "k" in this word.

Ec

Sometimes when "e" is followed by "c" it has the long "E" sound followed by a "k" sound.

eclipse   economics   economy

Ed

In most words where "e" is followed by "d", it has the short "e" sound followed by the "d" sound.

edge	edible	bed	federal	edifice
edit	medical	red	edition	
education	sled			

Ee

In almost every word with "ee" the double "e" sounds like the long "E" sound (The Chinese "i") .

eel	bee	feed	feel	greed
green	meet	need	seed	weed
wheel				

Ef

In most words that begin with "ef" you get the "short "e" sound followed by the "f" sound.

effective	effeminate	efficient	effort	definite
hefty	left	nefarious	referee	theft

Eg

Sometimes the letters "eg" have the short "e" sound followed by the hard "g" sound.

egg   beg   keg   leg   mega

If the "Eg" is followed by an "o", the "e" changes to the long "E" sound.

ego   egomania   egotism   egotistical

Ei and Eigh

In most cases, the letters "ei" and "eigh" make the long "A" sound.

eight   eighteen   eighth   feign   reign

weight

The exception to the rule is "either" and "neither" which in British English has the sound of the Chinese "ai" and in American English takes the sound of the long "E".

either   neither

Ej

In words beginning with "ej", the letters sound like the long "E" followed by the "j" sound.

ejaculate   eject   ejection

EL

Sometimes "EL" sounds like the short "e" followed by the "L".

elbow   elder   element elevate   elevator

Sometimes when words begin with "EL", it sounds like the long "E" followed by the "L" sound.

elaborate   elated   elect   electricity

elongated   elusive

Em

In most cases "em" sounds like the short "e" followed by the "m" sound.

embarrass   embassy   embezzle   embrace

embroidery   empire   employer   empty

hemisphere   temperament   temperature   unkempt

En

Sometimes the letters "en" sound like the short "e" followed by the "n" sound.

encourage   end   enemy   energy

engagement   engine   enjoy   enlarge

enter   environment

The exception to the rule is the word "English" where the "En" sounds like the long "E" followed by the "n" sound

English

Ep

In most cases the letters "ep" sound like the short "e" sound followed by the "p" sound.

Epic   epidemic   episode   epitaph   epitome

Equ

In most cases the letters "equ" sound like the long "E" followed by the "qu" sound which sounds something like "kwa" or "kwe".

equal   equator   equipment

equivocal

The exception to the rule is the words "equity" and "equitable" which both start with the short "e" sound, followed by the "qui" sound.

equity   equitable

Er

Sometimes the letters "er" sound like the word "air" when they are at the beginning of a word.

era   errand   error

Sometimes the letters "er" sound like the long "E" sound followed by the "r" sound when they are at the beginnings of words.

eradicate   erase   erect   erode   erotic

eruption

Usually when "er" is within a word, the letters sound like the soft "e" followed by the "r" sound.

Emperor   every   her   nervous   perfect

verve

"Er" makes the same sound as an ending to words.

camper   corner   dancer   father   gather

later   mother   never   prefer   temper

weather

Es

The letters "es" almost always make the sound of the short "e" followed by the "s" sound.

escape   essay   essential   establish

estimate (v) estimate (n)

Esh

The letters "esh" almost always sound like the short "e" followed by the "sh" sound.

fresh   mesh

Ess

The letters "ess" almost always sound like the short "e" followed by the "s" sound.

digress   distress   impress   mess   mistress

press

Est

The letters "est" almost always sound like the short "e" followed by the "st" sound.

best	crest	chest	guest	incest
nest	pest	rest	test	zest

Et

The letters "et" almost always have the sound of the short "e" followed by the "t" sound.

etch	bet	get	let	met
net	set	veteran		

However, the words "eternal" and "eternity" begin with the long "E" sound followed by the "t" sound.

eternal eternity

Eth

The letters "eth" almost always have the sound of the short "e" followed by the soft "th" sound. This is the "th" sound in the words "three" and "mouth".

ethereal	ethical	ethics	ethnicity

Eu

The letters "eu" sound like the long "u" with a "y" in front of it.

eulogy	eunuch	euphemism	Europe

Ev

Sometimes the letters "ev" sound like the short "e" followed by the "v" sound.

ever   everybody   everyone   evidence

evolution

But in most cases, the letters "ev" has the long "E" sound followed by the "v" sound.

evacuate   evaluate   evaporate   even

evening   event   eventual   evict

evil   evoke   evolve

Ew

In most cases, the letters "ew" have the sound of the long "U" followed by the "w" sound.

drew   few   grew   Jewish   new

stew   view

Ex

In almost every case, the letters "ex" sound like the short "e" sound followed by the "x" sound. This "x" sound is almost like a "g" followed by a "z" sound, like in the words "eggs".

exact   examine   example   exceed

exception   exchange   exclusive   excuse

executive	exempt	exercise	exhaust
exhibit	exist	expand	expense
experience	expert	explain	explore
explosion	export	expression	extend
extra			

Ey

The letters "ey" can sound like the Chinese "ai".

eye	eyeball	eyebrow	eyelash
eyelet	eyelid		

The letters "ey" can also sound like "ay" when contained within a word.

convey	grey	hey	prey

Ia

The letters "ia" together has many different sounds. It can sound like a long "E" followed by the short "a" sound.

piano

It can also sound like a long "E" followed by an "ah" sound.

fiancé   Fiat

It can also sound like a long "I" followed by a short "u" sound.

bias   trial   vial

Ib

The letters "ib" almost always sound like the short "i" sound followed by the "b" sound.

bib   crib   fib   nibble   rib

Tibet

As is usually the case, if there is an "e" after the "ib, the "i" is changed to a long "i" sound.

bible   bribe   fiber   tribe   vibe

Ic

The letters "ic" usually make the sound of the long "I" followed by a "k" sound.

icon   iconoclast

If the letters "ic" are followed by an "e", "I" or a "y", the "c" becomes the "s" sound.

ice   iceberg   ice cream   icicle   icing

icy

Ich

The letters "ich" usually end words and usually have the sound of the short "i" sound followed by the "ch" sound.

sandwich   which

Ick

The letters "ick" usually end words and usually have the sound of the short "i" sound followed by the "k" sound.

brick	chick	lick	nickel	quick
sick	trick			

Id

Sometimes the letters "id" sound like the short "i" followed by the "d" sound.

idiom	idiot	idiosyncrasy	bid
did	lid	rid	video

But most times if "id" starts a word, the sound is the long "I" followed by the "d" sound.

idea	identical	identity	ideology
idle	idolize		

If

In almost every word where you have the "if" sound, the "i" sound is the short "i" followed by the "f" sound.

if	different	drift	gift
lift	sift	stiff	whiff

If an "e" follows the "if", then the "i" sound generally becomes the long "i" sound.

life	knife	rifle	strife
trifle	wife		

38

Ig

In most cases, the letters "ig" sound like the short "i" sound followed by the hard "g" sound.

ignite	ignition	ignoble	ignorance	ignore
big	dig	figure	gigabyte	rig
swig	trigger			

IL

In most cases, the letters "il" (usually "ill" in words) has the short "i" sound followed by the "L" sound.

ill	illegal	illegitimate	illiterate	illogical
illustrate	bill	drill	fill	gill
hill	kill	mill	pill	swill
will				

Im

In almost every word containing the "im" sound, the "i" is the short "i" followed by the "m" sound.

imagine	imitation	immature	immediate	immune
impair	impersonate	impolite	import	

impractical	impress	imprint	improper
improve	dimple	limp	pimple
simple	shrimp	wimp	

In

In most words with the letters "in", the "i" sounds like the short "i" followed by the "n" sound.

in	inability	inaccurate	inadequate
insane	incense	inch	incident
incline	incoherent	income	incompatible
incompetent	incomplete	inconsistent	inconspicuous
inconvenient	incredible	indecent	indefinite
independent	indestructible	indicate	indifferent
indiscreet	individual	industry	infamous
infant	infect	infer	infest
infinite	inform	ingredient	inject injure
inquire	insect	insecure	insert
inside	insist	inspire	install
instant	instinct	instruct	insufficient
insult	intelligence	interior	internal
interview	intimate	into	introduce
invade	invention	invert	invest

invincible	inward	bin	chin
dinner	grin	pin	skin
spin	wird		

The exceptions to this rule are words where "in" is at the end of the word and followed by a "d". In most cases, the "i" then becomes the long "I" sound followed by the "nd" sound. "wind" has two pronunciations.

behind blind find grind kind mind unwind

Io

Sometimes the letters "io" sound like the long "I" sound followed by the long "O" sound.

| iodide | iodine | iota | diode | prior |

Sometimes the letters "io" sound like the long "I" sound followed by the short "o" sound.

| ion | ionic | bionic | lion |

If the "io" comes after a double "LL" and is followed by an "n" it usually sounds like "yun" with a short "u" sound.

| billion | billionaire | million | millionaire | rebellion |

Ip

In most words with the letters "ip" the "i" sounds like the short "i" sound followed by the "p" sound.

| blip | chip | cripple | dip | drip |
| flip | grip | hip | lip | quip |

| rip | ripple | ship | sip | strip |
| tip | trip | whip | | |

Ir

Sometimes the letters "ir" sound like the long "I" followed by the "r" sound.

| irate | Irish | irony |

Sometimes the letters "ir" sound like the short "e" sound followed by the "r" sound.

| chirp | dirt | girl | shirt | stir |
| swirl | whirl | | | |

The exception to the general "IR" rules is the word "iron", which sound like the long "I" followed by a "y" sound.

Iron

Irr

If a word begins with the letters "irr", it almost always sounds like the long "E" sound followed by the "r" sound.

| irrational | irregular | irresistible | irresponsible |

Is

The letters "is" usually sound like the short "i" sound followed by the "s."

disrespectful   misunderstand   whisper

Sometimes the letters "is" can sound like the short "i" sound followed by the "z" sound.

is Islam

The exception to the grammar rule with the letters "is" are the words "island" and aisle where the letters sound like the long "I" sound and the "s" is silent (not heard).

island   aisle

Ish

The letters "ish" usually sound like the short "i" followed by the "sh".

dish	fish	squish	swish	wish

Iss

The letters "iss" almost always sound like the short "i" followed by the "s" sound.

dismiss	kiss	miss	prissy	sissy

Ist

The letters "ist" sometimes sound like the short "i" followed by the traditional "st" sound.

distance	fist	list	mister	sister

twist

In some rare cases, the letters "ist" sound like the short "i" followed by the "s" sound, with the "t" being silent (not heard).

Christmas	listen	thistle	whistle

It

The letters "it" usually sound like the short "i" followed by the "t" sound.

it	Italian	itch	itself	Italy
bitter	hit	little	sit	

Sometimes the letters "it" sound like the long "I" followed by the "t" sound.

item	itinerary

Iv

Usually, the letters "iv" sound like the long "I" followed by the "v" sound, especially if the "v" is followed by an "e", an "o" or a "y".

ivory	ivy	alive	drive	knives
strive	wives			

But the exceptions to the rule are certain words where "iv" is followed by an "e" (or "o" in the case of pivot) where the "iv" sounds like the short "i" followed by the "v" sound.

give	live	liver	pivot	river
shiver	vivid			

Ix

The letters "ix" almost always sound like the short "i" followed by the true "x" sound (as in axe – not xylophone).

Dixie	fix	mixture	six	sixteen

sixty   vixen

Iz and Izz

The letters "iz" and "izz" always make the sound of the short "i" followed by the "z" sound.

dizzy   drizzle   fizz   fizzle   sizzle

tizzy   whiz

Oa

The letters "Oa" often make the long "O" sound.

oaf   oak   oat   afloat   boat

coat   encroach   goat   loaf   moan

roach   road   soap   toast

The exception to this rule is the word "Oasis" where both the "o" and the "a" are clearly pronounced.

oasis

If the letters "oa" are followed by an "r", then it sounds like the word "or".

oar   aboard   boar   board   hoard

roar   soar

Ob

Sometimes the letters "ob" sound like the short "o" sound followed by the "b" sound.

object	obnoxious	obscene	observe	obtain
obvious	job	knob	mobster	robber
throb				

Sometimes the letters "ob" sound like the long "o" followed by the "b" sound.

obedient	obese	oblige	obliterate	oboe

Oc and Occ

Sometimes "oc" and "occ" sound like the short "o" followed by the "k" sound.

occupation	occupy	octagon	October	octopus

Sometimes "oc" and "occ" sound like the long "O" sound followed by the "k" sound. It should be noted that Americans often pronounce these words with a short "u" sound instead of the long "O".

occasion	occult	occur	occurrence	o'clock

One exception to the rule is the word "ocean" and other words beginning with it. In these words the "oc" sounds like the long "O" followed by the "sh" sound.

ocean	oceanic	oceanography

Another exception is the word "ocelot" where the letters "oc" sound like the short "o" followed by the "s" sound.

ocelot

Ock

The letters "ock" always sound like the short "o" followed by the "k" sound.

dock	clock	lock	mock	rock

shock   stock

Od

Sometimes the letters "od" sound like the short "o" sound followed by the "d" sound.

odd   oddity   odyssey   body   modest

rod   sod

Sometimes the letters "od" sound like the long "O" sound followed by the "d" sound.

ode   odious   odor   podium   soda

sodium

Of and Off

With the exception of the word "of" which sounds like the short "u" sound followed by the "v" sound, the letters "of" and "off usually sound like the short "o" sound followed by the "f" sound.

off   offensive   offer   office   officer

offset   offshore   offspring   loft   often

profit   soft

And there are a few words where the letters "of" sound like the long "O" followed by the "f" sound.

offend   official   officiatep   rofanity

professional   profile   proficient   profusely   sofa

tofu

As you can see, with the exception of the word "profit", almost all words beginning in "prof" have the long "O" sound.

Og

The letters "og" usually sound like the short "o" sound followed by the hard "g" sound.

ogle	bog	dog	fog	hog
eggnog	soggy	toggle		

The exception to the rule is the word "ogre" which sounds like the long "o" followed by the hard "g" sound.

ogre

Oh

Sometimes the letters "oh" sound like the long "O" sound followed by the "h" sound.

Ohio	Soho	coherent	cohesion	cohort

The exceptions to this rule are the two words in the English language that begin with "Oh", oh and ohm. In these words the letters "oh" sound like the long "O" and the "h" is silent.

oh   ohm

Oi

Generally the letters "oi" sound like the letters "oy" in the words "boy" and "toy".

| oil | ointment | choice | hoist |
| invoice | moist | voice | |

OL

Usually the letters "ol" sound like the long "O" followed by the "l" sound.

old	oleander	olfactory	bold
bolt	cold	colt	control
dolt	gold	hold	mold
sold	told		

There are a few words where the letters "ol" sound like the short "o" followed by the "l" sound.

| oligarchy | olive | golf | solid |

In the words "wolf" and "wolves", the letters "ol" sound like a short "u" followed by the "f" sound.

| wolf | wolves |

Oll

Generally the letters "oll" sound like the short "o" followed by the "l". This sounds like the word "all".

| doll | dollar | follow | golly | holly |
| lollypop | mollusk | pollen | volley | |

Sometimes the letters "oll" sound like the long "O" followed by the "l" sound.

| knoll | poll | roll | stroll | toll |

49

troll

Om

Sometimes the letters "om" sound like the short "o" followed by the "m" sound.

omelet   ominous   omnipotent   omnivorous

Sometimes the letters "om" sound like the long "O" followed by the "m" sound.

omega   omen   omit

Sometimes the letters "om" sound like the short "u" sound followed by the "m" sound.

come   from   handsome   ransom

some

On

Sometimes the letters "on" sound like the short "o" sound followed by the "n" sound.

on   ongoing   onslaught   onward

Sometimes the letters "on" sound like the long "O" followed by the "n" sound.

only   phony   pony   stony

Sometimes the letters "on" sound like the short "u" followed by the "n" sound.

onion	carbon	done	honey	money
none	ton			

The exceptions to the standard rules are the words "one" and "once" where the "on" sounds like the "w" sound followed by the short "u" sound and the "n" sound.

one	once

Oo

Sometimes the letters "oo" sound like a long "U".

food	fool	spook	spooky
spool	spoon		

Sometimes the letters "oo" has a sound that is unique from other phonetic sounds. It sounds like the "oo" sound in the word "book".

crook	good	look	nook	shook
took	wood		

Op

Sometimes the letters "op" sound like the short "o" sound followed by the "p" sound.

opera	operate	operation	optic optimist
option	cop	drop	flop hop
mop	shop	stop	top

Sometimes the letters "op" sound like the long "O" sound followed by the "p" sound.

open   opener   openingopium

Opp

Usually, the letters "opp" sound like the short "o" followed by the "p" sound.

opportune   opportunity   opposite

dropping   hopping   mopping

shopper   stopper   topple

The exceptions to this are "opponent", "oppose" and "oppression" where the "o" sounds like the The short "u" followed by the "p".

opponent   oppose   oppression

Oar

The letters "oar" sound like the long "O" sound followed by the "a" sound, then the "r" sound.

oar   boar   board   hoard   roar

soar

Or

The letters "or" always sound like the word "or" which sounds the same as the word "oar".

or   oral   orange   oratory   orb

orbit	orchard	orchestra	orchid	ordeal
order	ordinal	ordinary	ore	organ
organic	organism	organize	orgy	Orient
Oriental	orientation	orifice	origin	original
originate	ornament	ornate	orphan	orthodox
adorn	bore	corn	for	glory
horn	lord	morning	sordid	torn

Os

Sometimes the letters "os" sound like the short "o" followed by the "s" sound.

oscillate   hospital

Osh

Almost always, the letters "osh" sound like the short "o" followed by the "sh" sound.

gosh   posh   slosh

Oss

Usually the letters "oss" sound like the short "o" followed by the "s" sound.

boss   emboss   floss   loss   moss

toss

Two exceptions to this rule are "engross" and "gross". Here, the letters "oss" sound like the long "O" followed by the "s" sound.

engross   engrossed   gross

Ost

Sometimes the letters "ost" sound like the short "o" followed by the "st" sound.

ostensible   ostracize   ostrich   lost   roster

Sometimes the letters "ost" sound like the long "O" followed by the "st" sound.

ghost   host   most

Ot

Usually the letters "ot" sound like the short "o" followed by the "t" sound.

dot   got   hot   lot   motley

not   rot   tot

Oth

The letters "oth" can sound like the short "o" followed by the soft "th" sound.

broth   cloth   gothic   moth   sloth

But the letters "oth" can also sound like the long "O" followed by the "th" sound.

both

The letters "oth" can also sound like the short "u" sound followed by the hard "th" sound.

other   otherwise   brother   mother

An exception to this rule is the word "nothing" which has the soft "th" sound.

nothing

Ott

The letters "ott" can sound like the short "o" sound followed by the "d" sound.

otter   bottle

The letters "ott" can also sound like the short "o" sound followed by the "t" sound.

forgotten   hotter   mottle   rotten

Ou

The letters "ou" sometimes sound like the sound made with "ow" as in the word "how".

ounce   our   oust   out

bout doubt gout hour   house joust loudlounge lout

mouse   pouch   pound   pout   round

route   sound   sour

But sometimes the letters "ou" when followed by a letter "r" can sound like "or".

tour   velour

Ous

The letters "ous" sound like the short "u" followed by the "s" sound.

delicious   delirious   famous hilarious   raucous

serious   stupendous   vicious victorious

Ouse

The letters "ouse" can also sound like the "ow" sound followed by the "s" sound.

house   mouse   spouse

Ov

Sometimes the letter "ov" can sound like the long "O" followed by the "v" sound.

oval   ovary   ovation   over

overcome   overdo   overflow   overhead

overlook   overnight   bovine   rove

rover   trove

But sometimes the letters "ov" can sound like the short "u" sound followed by the "v" sound.

oven   above   cover   coven   dove

glove   hover   love   shove

The exceptions to these rules are the words "approve" and "move" which sounds like the letters "oo" followed by the "v" sound.

approve move

Ow

The letter "ow" can sound like the "ow" in "how".

allow	bow	brow	cow	how
meow	now	sow	vow	wow

But it can also sound like the long "O" followed by the "w" sound.

owe	own	bow	bowtie	crow
know	low	row	mow	show
shown	tow			

Owl

The letters "owl" sound like the "ow" sound followed by the "L" sound.

owl	cowl	fowl	growl	howl

The exception to this rule is the word "bowl" which sounds like the long "o" sound followed by the "w" sound and the "L" sound.

bowl

Ox

The letters "ox" always sound like the short "o" sound followed by the "x" sound.

ox	oxidation	oxide	oxygen
box	fox	toxic	

Oy

The letters "oy" sound like the long "O" followed by the "y" sound.

oyster   alloy   boy   coy   soybean

toy

Oz

The letters "oz" sound like the long "O" followed by the "z" sound.

Ozone

Ua

The letters "ua" usually sound like the long "u" followed by the "w" sound.

Guava   quad   quadruplet   quart

quarter   square

The exceptions to the rule are the words "dual", "pursuant" and "truant" where the letters "ua" sound like the long "U" followed by the short "u".

dual   pursuant   truant

Ub

Sometimes the letters "ub" sound like the short "u" followed by the "b" sound.

bubble   cub   club   flub   grub

hub   nub   pub   public   rub

rubber	stub	stubble	subdue	subject
sublime	submarine	substitute	tub	

Sometimes the letters "ub" sound like the long "U" followed by the "b" sound. This is usually the way it sounds if the "b" is closely followed by another vowel.

dubious	jubilee	lubricate	puberty
pubescent	pubic	rubies	tubular

Uch

Usually the letters "uch" sound like the short "u" followed by the "ch" sound. For the same sound, also see "utch". They are identical. (also see utch)

much	such

Uck

Almost always, the letters "uck" sound like the short "u" followed by the "k" sound.

buck	buckle	duck	knuckle
lucky	muck	shuck	struck
stuck	suck	truck	tuck

Ud

Usually the letters "ud" sound like the short "u" followed by the "d" sound.

buddy	dud	huddle	mud	ruddy
stud	suds			

Uff

Almost always the letters "uff" sound like the short "u" followed by the "f" sound.

buff	duffle	fluff	gruff	huff
muffin	puff	suffer		

Ug

Usually the letters "ug" sound like the short "u" followed by the hard "g" sound.

ugly	bug	dug	hug	jug
lug	mug	rug	tug	

Ui

Sometimes the letters "ui" sound like the "w" sound followed by the short "i" sound.

penguin	quick	quip	quit	quilt
sequin				

Sometimes the letters "ui" sound like the long "U".

fruit	pursuit	recruit	suit

UL and ULL

Sometimes the letters "ul" will sound like the long "u" sound followed by the "L" sound.

Bull   full   July   pull

vestibule

Sometimes the letters "ul" will sound like the short "u" sound followed by the "L" sound.

Ulcer   ultimate   ultimatum   ultra

ultraviolet   cruller   dull   lullaby

null   sullen

Um

Sometimes the letters "um" sound like the short "u" sound followed by the "m" sound.

Umbrella   umpire   bum   gum   hum

jumble   mumble   number   rumble   strum

stumble   tumble

Umb

Sometimes when the letters "umb" are together, the "b" is silent. This is usually the way it sounds when the "b" is the last letter in the word.

Crumb   dumb   numb   thumb

Un

The letters "un" sometimes sound like the short "u" sound followed by the "n" sound.

Unable	unabridged	unacceptable
unattractive	unauthorized	unavailable
unavoidable	unaware	unbalanced
unbearable	unbelievable	unbroken
unbutton	uncertain	unchanged
uncivilized	unclean	unclear
uncomfortable	uncommon	uncut
undecided	undeniable	under
undergo	underground	underhanded
underline	underling	underneath
undernourished	underprivileged	understand
undivided	uneasy	uneducated
unemotional	unemployed	unequal
uneventful	unexplained	unfaithful
unfavorable	unfeeling	unfinished
unforgettable	unfriendly	ungrateful
unimaginative	unimportant	uninhabitable
unintelligent	unkind	unknowing

unlawful	unleash	unless
unlock	unlucky	unnatural
unnecessary	unpolished	unprofessional
unreal	unreasonable	unreliable
unsafe	unsuccessful	unsuitable
unsure	unthinkable	untidy
untie	until	unusual
unworthy	unwrap	unyielding
begun	bun	bungle
fun	gun	mundane
nun	plunder	pun
punish	run	sun
sundry	tunnel	

Sometimes the letters "un" sound like the "y" sound followed by the long "u" followed by the "n" sound. This is often the case when the "n" is followed by another vowel.

Unanimous	unicorn	uniform	unify
unilateral	union	united	unity
universal	university	funeral	

Up

The letters "up" usually sound like the short "u" sound followed by the "p" sound.

Up	upbringing	upgrade	uphill
uphold	uppermost	upright	uprising
uproot	upset	upstage	upstairs
cup	nuptials	rupture	suppress

Ur

Sometimes the letters "ur" sound like the short "u" followed by the "r" sound.

urban	urchin	urge	urgent	urn
ursine	burial	burn	burrow	fur
gurney	lure	mural	murky	plural
rural	turkey	turn		

Sometimes the letters "ur" sound like a "y" sound followed by a short "u" sound and then an "r" sound.

Uranium	Uranus	urethra	urinal	urinate
urine	cure	procedure	nurture	pure
torture				

Us

Sometimes the letters "us" sound like the short "u" followed by an "s" sound.

| bus | hustle | muscle | rustle | suspect |

Sometimes the letters "us" sound like a "y" sound followed by a long "U" sound and then an "s" sound. This is usually the case when a word begins with the letters "us".

Usable   usage   use   useful   usual

Ush

Sometimes the letters "ush" sound like the short "u" followed the "sh" sound.

Usher   brush   gush   hush   lush

mushroom   plush   rush   slush

Sometimes the letters "ush" sound like the long "u" sound followed by the "sh" sound.

Bush   cushion   push

Uss

Almost always, the letters "uss" will sound like the short "u" sound followed by the "s" sound.

Busses   cuss   fuss   mussed   tussle

Ust

Usually the letters "ust" sound like the short "u" followed by the "st" sound.

Bust   crust   custard   dust   gust

lust   mustard   rust   rustic   sustain

Utch

The letters "utch" always sound like the short "u" sound followed by the "ch" sound.

Clutch   Dutch   hutch

The only exceptions to this rule are the words "butch" and "butcher, where the "u" sounds like the "oo" sound in "book" and "look".

Butch   butcher

Uy

The letters "uy" usually sound like the Chinese "ai".

Buy   guy

Uzz

The letters "uzz" always sound like the short "u" followed by the "z" sound.

Buzz   buzzard   buzz-saw   fuzzy   muzzle

DIFFERENT PRONUNCIATIONS OF C

If a C is followed by an A, an O or a U, it almost always sounds like a K sound.

Cabin	cable	cactus	café	cake
calculate	calendar	calf	call	calm
camel	camera	can	candle	cap
capsule	captain	captive	car	card
care	carry	case	cash	casket
castle	catalog	cat	catch	cause
cave	coal	coat	cobra	coffee
coin	cold	collapse	collect	cologne
colonel	color	comb	combine	come
comedy	command	compact	comment	
companion	commit	company	commotion	compare
community	compass	compete	compile	
compliment	complete	complex	computer	comrade
concentrate	concept	concern	conclude	condemn
condition	cone	confess	confident	confirm

conflict	congratulate	connect	conserve	consider
console	conspicuous	constant	construct	consume
contain	contest	continue	contract	contrast
contribute	convenient	cub	cuddle	culture
cup	curb	cure	curl	current
curse	curtain	cut	cute	

Many times if a C is followed by an E, an I or a Y it will usually sound like S.

cedar	ceiling	celebrity	celery	cell
cement	center	centimeter	century ceramic	
cereal	ceremony	certain	cider	cigar
cigarette	cinema	cinnamon	circle	circuit
circumstance	circus	citadel	citizen	citrus
city	civilized	cyanide	cybernetics	cyborg
cycle	cyclone	cylinder	cymbal	cynic
cypress	cyst			

TWO SOUNDS FOR G

If the G is followed by an A, an O or a U, it generally sounds like the hard G as in gate, goal or gun.

Gadget	gallery	gamble	game	garden
gas	gather	going	gold	goodbye
goose	gorilla	government	gown	guard
guess	guide	guilty	guitar	gut
guy				

If the G is followed by an E, an I or a Y, it often sounds like J.

gee	gelatin	gem	general	
generation	generous	genie	genius	gentle
genuine	geography	geometry	germ	gin
ginger	giraffe	gist	gymnasium(gym)	
Gypsy	gyrate			

With "GI" the ratio of hard "G" sound to "J" sound is about 50 percent so you just have to learn the exceptions to this rule.

Get	giddy	gift	giggle	gill
gimmick	girdle	girl	give	

69

Other words with the "J" sound for G (pay attention to what letters follow the G)…

effigy   eulogy   magic   orange   prodigy

strategy   tragic

GH

Gh together has a few different sounds.

One is the hard "G" sound and the H is silent and basically serves no purpose.

ghastly   ghetto   ghost   ghoul

GH can also make the "F" sound.

cough   rough   tough

And in some cases it makes no sound at all.

bought   caught   sleigh   taught

though   through

KN

"KN" usually sounds like the "N" sound. The "K" is silent.

knee   kneel   knelt   knock   knot

know   knuckle

Though confusing, there is a reason for the K as many of these words have doubles (nee = born, no & not = negative).

I am not sure why the Queen's English initiated this rule for the other words as they could easily be understood without the K on the front (neel, nelt, nock, nuckle).

PH

"PH" is not based on vowel sounds but I felt it was important to mention that it usually sounds like "F".

phone	phonetics	phonics	physical
autograph	elephant	telegraph	telephone

THE TROUBLE WITH "V" AND "TH"

Something else that I wanted to share with you that is very important – Many of my students face this same problem. ZH in the Chinese language forms the sound that is the "J" in English like in the word "jacket". In the Chinese phonetic alphabet, the letters "X" and "Q" make the sound of "CH" like in the English word "children". However, the common English sounds that are NOT in the Chinese phonetic alphabet are the English letters "TH", "V" and the English "X".

It is very important that you practice extra hard on words with "TH" and "V". These are the sounds that get little practice in China as they are not in your phonetic alphabet. You never learned them from when you were a child.

If you do not practice these sounds, your mind will automatically pick the closest sound that it can find in your memory that can replace the original sound which it does not know well. This is why so many Chinese people who are just starting to learn English accidentally mispronounce a "V" as a "W". Be careful not to say "wolume" when you actually mean to say "volume."

Here are some "V" words to help you:

PRACTICE PRONUNCIATION

vacation	vagrant	valley	valiant	value
valuable	valve	vampire	vandal	vane
vanilla	vanish	variety	varnish	vegetable
vehicle	velvet	vendor	vengeance	venom
vent	verb	vermin	verse	vertical

vest	vibrate	vicious	victim	victory
video	view	village	vinegar	violate
violence	violin	virtual	virus	visa
vision	vital	vitamin	vivid	
vocabulary	voice	volcano	volume	volunteer
vote	voucher	vow	voyage	vulture

And words with "v" in them.

invaluable	inverted	invest	investment	invitation
invite	invoice			

A funny (strange) thing that I have noticed with my Chinese English students is that they all seem to be able to pronounce the word "very" well. Students who have trouble pronouncing "V" usually do not have a problem with it when they say "very". So, when you are practicing your "V"s, try saying the word "very" right before you say the other "V" words. It might help you to shorten your practice time.

"TH" actually has two sounds. A hard "TH" sound like in the word "There" and a softer "TH" sound like in the word "Three".

You might easily substitute an "S" sound for the softer "TH" sound in words. I hear people say "Sink" instead of "Think", "Sum" instead of Thumb", "Mouse" when they actually mean "Mouth". The "Z" sound and "D" sound are common substitutes for the hard "TH" sound. Students often say 'Zis", "Zat" and "Zose" as well as "Dis", "Dat" and "Dose" instead of "This", "That" and "Those". This is very common in China. Try not to fall into that trap.

With both "TH" sounds you should bring your tongue through your teeth and gently bite down on the tongue, when the sounds are made, you release your grip on the tongue, letting the tongue slip back into your mouth.

Practice making these sounds in front of a mirror.

PRACTICE PRONUNCIATION

Hard TH

this	that	those	these	theirs

although

Soft TH

three	throw	threw	with	mouth
teeth	think	through	thoroughly	

Another pronunciation mistake that I hear in my classes (though not as big a problem in China as "V's" and "TH's" but more of a problem in Japan) is the reversal of "R's" and "L's" when speaking English.

This can be especially embarrassing for you if you mispronounce someone's name. My name is "Rory". Can you imagine how many of my friends and students mispronounced my name when they first met me. I have been called "Wowy", "Rolly", "Lolly", and many other things.

Again, it is nothing to be embarrassed about. It is not your fault that these sounds are not in the Chinese alphabet. The answer to this problem is simple – practice, practice, practice.

PRACTICE VOCABULARY

Radar	Rage	Railroad	Rainbow	Rally
Ramble	Rapture	Rare	Rattle	Reading
Realistic	Rear	Recall	Receipt	Recent

Reception	Recognize	Record	Recover	Recreation
Recruit	Rectangle	Reduce	Refill	Reflex
Refrigerator	Regard	Regret	Regular	Rejuvenate
Relative	Relaxing	Reliable	Relief	Reorganize
Repair	Reply	Reproduce	Reserved	Resort
Reservoir	Restaurant	Retire	Retrieve	Return
Revolver	Rhinoceros	Rhythm	Ridiculous	Ringleader
Roar	Rolling	Rooster	Rough	Royal
Rubber	Ruffle	Rumble	Runway	Rural
Ruthless				

There is a famous story that Chinese Kung-Fu legend Bruce Lee (Li Xiao Leung) liked to tell. According to Lee, in 1966 he got his first big role as "Kato" on an American television show called "The Green Hornet", not due to his being handsome or his incredible fighting style, but because he was the only Asian actor at the audition who could pronounce the show's leading character's names correctly. The names were… The Green Hornet and Britt Reid, both containing "R" sounds. While his pronunciation was near perfect, other actors were saying Gleen Hohnet and Blitt Leid.

Now that you are more familiar with how the phonetics make English words sound, we can move on to practicing our English speaking. It is time to start opening your mouth and speaking English words, phrases, and sentences.

ARTICULATION

Phonetics are important to good English, but excellent articulation is what is going to make what you say easy for people to understand. Articulation is the way you open your mouth and say words.

Bad articulation, such as poor voice volume, people mumbling and/or not speaking clearly, is the biggest cause of communication breakdown. Communication is lost when someone says something and the person they are saying it to, does not hear it or understand it.

In my classes, I like to use "tongue twisters" to help my students to practice opening their mouths and speaking quickly. If you do a word search on the internet for "tongue twisters" you will find thousands of sites dedicated to them. They are fun and are supposed to be spoken fast... the faster the better.

Most people stumble and stammer while trying to say tongue twisters the first few times. It is alright. They were created for that purpose. After you practice using your tongue twisters, you will find yourself getting better and better at reciting them. As the old proverb tells us, "Practice makes perfect". That is definitely true with tongue twisters. Once you master them, you can impress your friends and classmates by quickly saying them. It will build your confidence and also help you with your articulation.

"TONGUE TWISTERS"

Here are a few sample tongue twisters that you can practice. Remember, the faster you say them, the more they will help you with your articulation. Say them as fast as you can.

SHE SELLS SEASHELLS BY THE SEASHORE.

RUBBER BABY BUGGY BUMPERS.

THE BLACK BACKED BAT BIT BACK.

I WISH TO WASH MY IRISH WRISTWATCH.

WHICH WRISTWATCHES ARE SWISS WRISTWATCHES?

IF STU CHEWS SHOES. SHOULD STU CHOOSE THE SHOES THAT HE CHEWS.

A BIG BLACK BUG BIT A BIG BLACK DOG ON HIS BIG BLACK NOSE.

TIE TWINE TO THREE TREE TWIGS.

SEVENTY-SEVEN BENEVOLENT ELEPHANTS.

THREE SHORT SWORD SHEATHS.

SIX SLEAK SWANS SWAM SWIFTLY SOUTHWARD.

WHEN YOU WRITE COPY, YOU HAVE THE RIGHT TO COPYRIGHT THE COPY YOU WRITE.

THE GREEN QUEEN SEEMED TO SCREAM.

TOM THREW TIM THREE THUMTACKS.

SIX SLICK SNAKES SLID SLOWLY AND SILENTLY.

YELLOW LEATHER, BLACK LEATHER, GREEN LEATHER, RED LEATHER, BLUE LEATHER, ORANGE LEATHER, BROWN LEATHER, ETC.

HOW CAN YOU CRAM A CLAM INTO A CLEAN CREAM CAN?

STUPID SUPERSTITION!

RED BULB, BLUE BULB, RED BULB, BLUE BULB.

DOUBLE BUBBLE GUM, BUBBLES DOUBLE.

PURPLE PAPER PEOPLE, PURPLE PAPER PEOPLE.

AN APE HATES GRAPE CAKES.

A SKUNK SAT ON A STUMP. THE STUMP THOUGHT THE SKUNK STUNK.

I THOUGHT A THOUGHT, BUT THE THOUGHT I THOUGHT WASN'T THE THOUGHT I THOUGHT I THOUGHT.

ANN SENT ANDY TEN HENS AND ANDY SENT ANN TEN PENS.

BLAKE THE BAKER BAKES BLACK BREAD.

UNIQUE NEW YORK

TOY BOAT, TOY BOAT, TOY BOAT.

SAM'S SHOP STOCKS SHORT SPOTTED SOCKS.

VINCENT VOWED FOR VENGEANCE AND VICTORY.

SIX STICKY SUCKER STICKS.

SUNSHINE CITY. SUNSHINE CITY.

GIVE POPPA A PROPER CUP OF COFFEE IN A COPPER COFFEE CUP.

DON'T PAMPER DAMP TRAMPS THAT CAMP UNDER RAMP LAMPS.

THE SAWINGEST SAW I EVER SAW WAS THE SAW I SAW IN ARKANSAS.

SHREDDED SWISS CHEESE.

The most famous of all tongue twisters is Peter Piper. It is a popular verse in many countries.

PETER PIPER

PETER PIPER PICKED A PECK OF PICKLED PEPPERS.

HOW MANY PICKLED PEPPERS DID PETER PIPER PICK?

IF PETER PIPER PICKED A PECK OF PICKLED PEPPERS,

WHERE'S THE PECK OF PICKLED PEPPERS PETER PIPER PICKED?

This one takes a lot of practice. It helps if you remember that the correct order of the tongue twister is HOW, IF and WHERE.

This concludes your phonetics training. Practice your phonetics regularly, paying special attention to the sounds that you never learned (TH, V, X) because they are not in the Chinese alphabet.

What you have also gotten from this book is a lengthy list of new vocabulary.

LEAVE A REVIEW

I would be extremely grateful if you could take just a minute to write a review on Amazon about this book. Even if the review is brief (2 or 3 sentences) that would be incredibly helpful. Recommending this book to a friend doesn't hurt either :)

Thank you and I love you!!!

Please visit Amazon to leave a review.

ABOUT THE AUTHOR

Rory Penland has been writing for over 35 years. He has written skits, short stories, screenplays, and novels. Jon Fedkiw, head of "Just Write!" of Central Florida, calls Penland "one of the hardest working and most talented writers that Florida has to offer." Penland is also an established stand-up comedian, accomplished actor, professional singer, and artist.

While living in Tampa, Florida, he hosted a public access, live call-in TV show entitled "It's Casual," twice awarded the top award for "Entertainment Show in the Tampa Bay Area."

In 2002, Penland's screenplay Deadly Species was produced and was distributed by Artisan Films. Since that time, he has written a dozen other screenplays, all of which he is shopping now to various movie studios.

Penland spent 15 years living in Shenzhen in The People's Republic of China. While there, he worked as a clean-up artist for Jade Animation where he worked on the Disney animated show "Super Robot Monkey Team Hyper Force Go!" as well as Canada's "Biker Mice From Mars."
Penland is currently writing stories for The Tales of The Vampyr and Post-Apocalyptic Bachelor's Guides series of books.

ALSO AVAILABLE FROM PALM CIRCLE PRESS:

THE ATROCITY BELLS

The Lost Books of Jyn, Book One
Lee Anderson

*Immerse yourself in the captivating **Lost Books of Jyn**, a literary mystery that has fascinated scholars for generations. Both books contain a vivid narrative that whisks readers away to a supernatural world inhabited by kings and queens, men and monsters, warriors and warlocks.*

To learn more, click visit www.palmcirclepress.net today!

THE MOST BEAUTIFUL INSANITY

South Beach Crime Thriller Series, Book One
Heather Wilde

*(Wilde's) unusual lyricism stamps her characters and their sordid choices with authenticity. The result is an insider's lens on the grislier truths behind beauty and privilege."***The Miami Herald**

The fashion world is turned upside-down with the overdose death of a young wannabe. Police scrutiny exposes the debauchery of today's modeling biz...

To learn more, click visit www.palmcirclepress.net today!

THE VAMPIRE IRREGULARS

Book One in The Tales of the Vampyr Series
Rory Penland

Prepare to have your preconceptions shattered and your perception of vampires forever altered...

In the murky realm of the undead, where secrets abound and darkness reigns, a select few stand defiantly against the shadows. Amidst a backdrop of veiled existence, emerges "The Vampire Irregulars," a gripping anthology of enigmatic tales, divulged to the intrepid Timothy Janusch—a chronicler of the damned, and a bloodsucker in his own right.

To learn more, click visit www.palmcirclepress.net today!

DARK LORDS OF THE TRAILER PARK

Short Stories
Lee Anderson

Dark Lords of the Trailer Park

Short Stories
by Lee Anderson

Bathed in a relentless vision of moral decay, a gallery of captivating souls
emerges—beautiful losers, smooth criminals, and deranged lovers.

Bound by their unyielding determination, they navigate the labyrinth of their
existence with a bruised grace, seeking redemption amidst the most
unlikeliest of places.

To learn more, click visit www.palmcirclepress.net today!

WHAT HAPPENED AT SISTERS CREEK

A Horror Novel
Lee Anderson

A small town sherrif sends a search party into the woods to hunt two escape convicts. What they find instead is a savage, unthinkable horror...

"I squirmed, I cringed, I gritted my teeth and held my breath...And that ending.... I just.... WHAT? I don't even know what to say. Amazing? Exhilarating? Total WTF moment? It was soooooo good!" Jessica Scurlock, author of **Pretty Lies**

"It was VISCERAL for me as a reader in a way that all great horror/thrillers are. You want to be in it and at the same time you want to run the hell away from it as fast as you can!" Amanda Nicole Ryan, author of **Keeper**

To learn more, click visit www.palmcirclepress.net today!

BACHELOR'S GUIDE TO POST-APOCALYPTIC SUCCESS

Book One of the Post-Apocalyptic Bachelor Guides
Rory Penland

The Bachelor's Guide to Post-Apocalyptic Success

Book One of The Apocalyptic Bachelor Guides

Rory Penland

In the aftermath of humanity's annihilation, the quest for love becomes an arduous battle...

Brandon Hoffner, a once-renowned baseball star turned resilient entrepreneur, emerges from cryo-sleep to a desolate wasteland, a world ravaged by the merciless jaws of a nuclear holocaust. In a landscape where hope teeters on the precipice of extinction, Hoffner's quest transcends the boundaries of mere companionship. He yearns not only for human connection but also for the possibility of perpetuating the dwindling flame of the human race.

To learn more, click visit www.palmcirclepress.net today!